STILL LIFE
IN
IMPRESSIONISM

PARK
LANE

Still Life in Impressionism

Still life, as a pictorial genre, spread throughout Europe from the eighteenth century onwards. However, the term only came into current usage during the nineteenth century, when it expressed the disdain of Classicism for a genre which it considered to be a servile imitation of the most insignificant reality. Nevertheless, still life has a very ancient tradition, whose origins go back to the Hellenistic age. It is only from the sixteenth century, and during late Mannerism, that one can speak of an autonomous genre, deriving from the grotesques of the Neronian era and the mosaic flooring of late Roman imperialism. Thus, paintings of flowers, fruit, musical instruments, game and fish came into being and became popular, following both a pictorial and a philosophical con-

1 – Jean-François Millet. *Primroses* – 1868. Museum of Fine Arts, gift of Quincy Adams Shaw, intermediaries Q.A. Shaw Jr. and Mrs. Marian Shaw Haughton, Boston.

2 – Henri Fantin-Latour. *Still Life* – 1869. Musée des Beaux-Arts, Grenoble.

3 – Henri Fantin-Latour. *Narcissi and Tulips* – 1862. Musée du Louvre, Paris.

ception. This conception represented the evolution and change in human conscience and the organisation of and compensation for the daily tasks in life, its interests, anxieties and desires, in a temporal perspective dominated by a knowledge of the transience of human existence, of *vanitas*; so that the skull, the hourglass and the faded flowers, placed alongside objects evoking the richness and joy of the senses, also became *memento mori*.

Modern still life developed at the time of Flemish Realism and was encouraged by the profane tendencies which entered painting after the Protestant iconoclasm. In a true revolution of themes, large displays of vegetables or meat took over the foreground of paintings, relegating human figures to the background. With great descriptive detail the Dutch painters presented food and objects, beautifully arranged on dining-room tables, on market stalls or on collector's shelves. These Dutch still lifes, more precisely defined by the term "still-leven" (tranquil, immobile life), were designed for the houses

5 – Edouard Manet. *Bar at the Folies-Bergères* – 1881-82. Courtauld Institute Galleries, London.

4 – Edouard Manet. *Vase of Peonies* – 1864. Musée du Louvre, Paris.

of rich merchants who loved to surround themselves with lifelike images of their material wealth.

In the eighteenth century, still life took a decorative role, and the best results were achieved by Jean-Baptiste Chardin in whose work the tranquil life of objects reached a highpoint of intimacy and purity. The neo-classical reaction to painting of this kind led to a decline of still life, which many nineteenth century romantic painters only rarely practised.

However, the impressionist painters, particularly Cézanne, were to bring the genre back to the centre of artistic experience. In their eyes, flowers, fruit, animals, washing, and objects of everyday use carried the same importance and the same dignity as the human figure. They were inspired by Dutch seventeenth-century painting, whose sharp and precise power of observation they admired. However, contrary to the Dutch painters, who tended to provide a sense of harmony within a balanced arrangement and who classified objects according to the spectator, the Impressionists implied the presence of an observer within the composition-space containing the still life.

Painting isolated objects or objects within a portrait or within paintings of interiors, the Impressionists depicted the symbols of social life and, as chroniclers of their time, they also left an important testimony of still life.

One of the direct predecessors of the Impressionists was Jean-François Millet (1814-1875). Born in Normandy, where he spent his childhood, he received a religious education which gave him an austere conception of life and a pessim-

6 – Edouard Manet.
*Bunch of Peonies and Pruning
Scissors* (detail) – 1864.
Musée du Louvre, Paris.

7 – Edouard Manet. *Stems of
Peonies and Secateurs* – 1864.
Musée du Louvre, Paris.

istic vision of the world. On his arrival in Paris, where he studied with Delacroix, he settled in Barbizon, a village in the forest of Fontainebleau, in 1849. A group of painters, whose aim was to work away from the conventional academic circles, had settled there and were often joined by the Impressionists. He worked in close contact with Théodore Rousseau, revealing a sensibility and spiritualism which prompted him to paint subjects inspired by agricultural labour. In the country, alongside peasants who worked long and hard in the fields, he also discovered the splendour of nature, as depicted in *Primroses* (plate 1), a pastel work of 1868 which demonstrates his qualities as a draughtsman, wisely highlighting the pale colours of the flowers against the sombre, wooden background.

The Batignolles Studio

Although coming from very different backgrounds and having different temperaments, all the avant-garde artists knew each other and formed friendships during the years between 1860 and 1870, contributing, each in his own way, to the formation of the movement that later came to be known as Impressionism. They met in their studios, frequented Parisian cafés, and travelled through France – all, or nearly all, with very limited financial resources – searching for ideal places to paint. They all felt the desire to liberate their personality through a direct contact with nature and with life, and to break all academic conventions. Their teachers, Gleyre, Lehmann, Lamotte and Couture, were more or less mediocre artists, who had all become famous as students of the great masters of Classicism, such as David or Ingres. They had spread the word of Classicism, constantly repeated in fixed, dogmatic formulas, and empty of any profound or original meaning.

These young painters, thirsty for new experiences, rebelled against it all.

In 1863, in Gleyre's studio, a first group of Impressionists was formed, bringing together students linked by friendship and the same affinity of ideas – Renoir, Monet, Sisley and Bazille. In 1865 and 1866 the meetings held at the Café Guerbois strengthened their links with Pissarro – which had only been sporadic until then – and with the group of artists and literary men who, a few years later, were to form the core of the impressionist group. After the Franco-Prussian war of 1870, which scattered the group of friends (some painters fled abroad, others were mobilised), two groups were formed: the first centred around Monet, at Argenteuil, with whom Renoir, Sisley and the reticent Manet worked; the second at Pontoise, where Pissarro and Cézanne continued their research, side by side.

Manet is considered a leader of the school and was depicted as such by Fantin-Latour in his famous picture of the Batignolles studio, where Manet is surrounded by Renoir, Astruc, Maître, Bazille, Monet and Scholderer.

Two paintings by Henri Fantin-Latour (1836-1904), who was born in Grenoble and was a student of Courbet and later a friend of the Impressionists, are emblematic of the change which took place within the impressionist movement. The first, *Narcissi and Tulips* of 1862 (plate 3), still reveals the influence of seventeenth-century painters, who used a dark

8 – Edouard Manet. *Still Life with Grapes and Figs* – 1864. Mme Florence Gould Collection, Cannes.

background as a fundamental theme of their compositions. The wise introduction of the table top gives it a definite sense of movement and of depth.

As years went by, Fantin-Latour's palette became lighter, in line with the development of the other impressionist painters. In his *Still Life* of 1869 (plate 2), taken from nature at close quarters, he organised the effect of coloured textures with great precision: the velvety texture of the fruit, the transparency of the glass, the translucent opacity of the porcelain, the splash of colour of a variety of different flowers.

Edouard Manet

Strangely enough, the date of the death of Manet, one of the founders of Impressionism, coincides with the break-up and the dispersion of the first group of Impressionists. He was

white dress, next to a large straw hat, is an upturned basket of fruit, bread, red cherries on a bed of green leaves, and a bottle.

Still life had always been a focal point of Manet's art. He considered it an important genre in painting, as much when he was making a painting of flowers and fruit as when he inserted them into his larger compositions. In 1868, he had introduced another still life into a painting, the *Lunch in the Studio*, at present in the Bayerische Staatsgemäldesammlungen in Munich.

Here, too, the objects assume the same importance as the people. Three people are represented around a table, set for lunch. We see Léon Koalla, known as Léonoff and probably the son of Manet, leaning on the edge of the table in the centre of the painting. In his black jacket he stands out clearly

9 – Edouard Manet. *Luncheon on the Grass* (detail) – 1863. Musée d'Orsay, Paris.

born in Paris on 23 January 1832, into a wealthy bourgeois family. His father was a magistrate; his mother the daughter of a well-known diplomat in Stockholm. In 1850, he joined the studio of Thomas Couture, which he would only leave six years later. He often went to the Louvre, where he tirelessly copied the ancient masters. In 1863 he presented his latest creation at the Salon des Refusés, *Luncheon on the Grass* (plate 10), which transformed the sixteenth-century "concerts champêtres" into a modern setting. This painting attracted a large public, scandalised by a naked woman sitting calmly between two men, fully-dressed from head to toe. In the foreground, on the left, a still life (plate 9) forms an integral part of the composition and serves to represent the start of the action taking place in the picture. The model has undressed before sitting down and on her light-blue dotted

against the grey background. Behind him, a maid holds a carafe and, on the right, a man sitting down and half-hidden by his hat, smokes a cigar. The melody of the still life flows over the continuous grey note of the background and the different elements capture the light in gleams, reflections, and droplets, in the Dutch manner. On the left there is a helmet, ancient arms and a large white vase with a plant. On the right, on a white cloth, painstakingly detailed in the squares and folds of its material, a transparent glass reflects the light. Oysters, a cut lemon, a knife, a bottle and a sugar

10 – Edouard Manet. *Luncheon on the Grass* – 1863. Musée d'Orsay, Paris.

11

bowl all demonstrate the vibrant liveliness of this composition and the harmony of its colours.

During the prolific years of production which preceded his "light period," Manet, in a variety of experimental studies, examined both still life and the great masters of painting from the past. The paintings done after 1856 show the influence of Velasquez. In *Guitar and Hat* (plate 11) of 1862, some touches of colour and a splash of white are enough to obtain superb results. He learnt from Velasquez that the greatest colourists are those who know how to limit their palettes. In still life he adopted a dark background as a fundamental theme of his compositions, but, thanks to the vibrant contrast by which the forms stand out, the background acquires a brilliant and limpid hue.

Whereas in the large paintings his fragile nervous system made it difficult for him to maintain a sense of spontaneity, in the still lifes, painted on inspiration, one notices no such uncertainty. Manet, like other painters of the period, knew how to make masterpieces from apparently very simple subjects, like flowers. It was a skilled stylistic exercise which many Impressionists undertook. Manet preferred to represent the triumph of bright flowers in his still lifes – roses, lilacs, peonies – and there are always touches of white, a colour which, like black, Manet regarded as equally important as all the others. During the summer of 1864 he made several still lifes: *Vase of Peonies* (plate 4), *Bunch of Peonies and Pruning Scissors* (plate 6), *Grapes and Figs* (plate 8), *Still Life, Fruit on a Table* (plate 13). If this last painting is overbur-

dened with a heavy and over-analytical touch, the *Vase of Peonies* is made with light, joyous brushstrokes, in a marvel of grace and goodness.

The red of the peonies in the background, retouched and with thicknesses of madder lacquer, has maintained its colour unaltered over time, even though Manet was suspicious of red and used it very sparingly. "Japanism and Hispanism, these are my sources, but my aim is to paint something modern," were Manet's words. It is not by chance that he introduced Japanese works into his *Portrait of Emile Zola* (plate 12) of 1867-68. In this way he combined both oriental and western traditions in a single work. The arrangement of the objects placed one behind the other, in parallel layers, is reminiscent of the principles of oriental composition and the dark colouring dominates the portrait, following the tradition of the ancient masters.

The desk – resembling a still life with books, manuscripts, a goose feather, a paper-knife and a catalogue containing the inscription "E. Manet" – is surmounted by a Japanese print of Utamaro, an engraving of *Los borrachos* by Velasquez and a reproduction of *Olympia* by Manet himself. The light, accentuated by the great black mass of Zola's jacket, guides the eye towards this magnificent still life, which even seems to acquire the same importance as the figure himself.

The *Portrait of Emile Zola* represents his farewell to the "black period", and Manet then began his conversion to light-coloured, paintings. He worked frenetically, although beginning to feel the first crises of illness in his left foot, a

11 – Edouard Manet. *Guitar and Hat* – 1862. Musée Calvet, Avignon.

12 – Edouard Manet. *Portrait of Emile Zola* – 1868. Musée d'Orsay, Paris.

13 – Edouard Manet. *Still Life, Fruit on a Table* – 1864. Musée d'Orsay, Paris.

sign of the ataxia which killed him. In May 1880 he went to Bellevue for hydrotherapy, which the doctors had prescribed for him. He stayed there for five months, and, in order to pass the time, he painted still lifes and landscapes. These spontaneous creations helped him to rest from the great effort of composition *Basket of Flowers* (plate 14).

In spite of his illness and suffering, Manet was very active and worked on the *Bar at the Folies-Bergères* (plate 5), which was exhibited with great success at the Salon in 1882. Here the painter introduced one of his most beautiful still lifes. Her two hands leaning on the bench, the barmaid provides a vertical form dividing the painting perfectly into two. On one side of the bench, there are bottles of spirits and champagne reflected in the mirror and, on the other side, a glass containing two roses, a crystal cup with oranges, and, further along, bottles "cut off" by the frame. A large mirror reflects the barmaid, the man speaking to her and the room full of people. Within the framework of the painting the still life comes to the fore, as real as the barmaid, while the rest of the painting is merely a reflection of reality.

In spite of the illness menacing Manet, he continued to paint until he was too weak to carry on. From July to October 1882 he had rented a house at Rueil and, lacking any other subject-matter, he painted splendid still lifes, pastels and small, more manageable oils, like the *Flowers in a Crystal Vase* now at the National Gallery of Art in Washington, which he offered as a New Year's gift to an unknown woman. In strange contrast with his declining health, the painting is a joyful celebration of the liveliness of nature: a bouquet of roses, carnations and pansies arranged haphazardly in a crystal vase.

Towards the middle of March 1883 his illness left him no respite. On the 20th, he had his left leg amputated to stop the gangrene. He died after 20 days of agony.

Edgar Degas

Edgar Degas had numerous points in common with Manet. They both came from upper middle-class families, and both were charmed by the novelty of Japanese art in its decorative freshness, its ironic and playful decomposition, and the rapid contrasts between light and dark tones. Just like Manet, Degas loved to insert still life into his portraits.

Edgar de Gas, the correct spelling of his name, which he used until about 1873, was born in Paris on 19 July 1834 into a cosmopolitan family. His father, a rich banker, was the son of a French exile, expatriate in Naples during the Revolution, and an Italian. His mother was a Creole from New Orleans. At eighteen, Degas received his father's permission to give up his academic studies in order to devote his time to painting. At first, his bourgeois upbringing directed his initial studies towards the more traditional artistic group, that of Ingres. He alternated his studies at the Louvre, where he copied the works of the ancient masters, with lessons, first from Louis Lemothe, then at the Ecole des Beaux-Arts. It was, in fact, at the Louvre, in 1862 that he met Manet for the first time. Coming from the same social background and having undertaken similar artistic training, they soon became very close friends and Degas started to frequent the cafés where the Impressionists met. However, he stayed aloof from their ideas, even when, in 1865, he presented his last historical painting, entitled *Les malheurs de la ville d'Orléans* with them at the Salon Officiel. From this year onwards he moved towards portraiture and scenes from contemporary life. In the superb family portraits, he introduced everyday objects which he animated with the same vitality as his human figures.

The figures are seen among the furniture and the objects which formed their familiar setting. Some details, such as the design of the wallpaper or the sculpted frame of a painting hanging on the wall, are shown as vividly as in a Dutch painting, as in *The Bellelly Family*, completed in 1859. Manet appreciated the painting for the audacity of its composition, but he disapproved of the representation of historical themes, a favourite subject of the Ecole des Beaux-Arts, which limited itself to commemorative themes of this type.

After the reopening of the Japanese market, the first prints started to arrive in France. In 1862 a shop opened, called "La Porte Chinoise," which was frequented by writers and painters like Manet, Monet and Degas. Going beyond the romantic exoticism of the Orient, Degas looked for the inner meanings in Japanese art which could conform to his studies. The asymmetry of the frame, the allusions, the unbalanced figures cut off by the edge of the picture led the spectator to a direct and intimate vision, as in *A Woman with Chrysanthemums*

14 – Edouard Manet. *Basket of Flowers* – 1880. Private collection.

15 – Camille Pissarro. *Roses from Nice* – 1902. Private collection.

(plate 16) of 1865. The model is shown in a natural and casual pose, unaware of the painter and she is confined to the extreme right section of the picture. In the middle of the picture there is a huge bunch of coloured chrysanthemums which limit the importance of the figure.

Another lively and spontaneous portrait, in which attention is drawn towards the objects and furniture all around, is the *Portrait of Hortense Valpinçon* (plate 17) of 1869. Degas created a contrast between the young girl in her simple white dress and the joyous and gaily-coloured designs of the carpet and the material on the table, reminiscent of the floral decorations of oriental lacquer ware.

After the Franco-Prussian war, during which he served in a Parisian fortress, and after a period spent in the country at the house of his Valpinçon friends during the Commune, Degas returned to Paris and started to frequent the Opera milieu, painting the world of ballet, which found in him its most poetic and most willing eulogist.

From 1886 his spiritual and intellectual isolation became a physical one, too. Problems with his sight grew and, at the same time, he became more and more morose. He dedicated himself to pastels, engravings and sculptures, using the eye of his memory with confidence and complete technical mastery. As solitary as he had been all his life, he retired to Saint-Valéry-sur-Sonne, where he ended his days. He died on 27 December 1917.

16 – Edgar Degas. *A Woman with Chrysanthemums* – 1865. The Metropolitan Museum of Art, H.O. Havemeyer Collection, New York.

Claude Monet

It was Claude Monet who painted, in 1872, *Impression, Sunrise*, prompting the critic Leroy to ironically use "Impressionism" as a definition of the work of this group of painters.

He was one of the first painters to experiment with effects of light, looking at nature with freshness and spontaneity, free from all the cultural superstructure of academic teaching. Oscar, as he was called by his family, started his artistic career as a caricaturist, and the caricatures which he painted of his fellow citizens in Le Havre have become famous. His family, originally from Paris, settled in Le Havre in 1845, when little Oscar was only five years old.

A painter from the town, Eugène Boudin, convinced Monet to train seriously to be an artist and, when he was nineteen, Claude moved to Paris with a letter of presentation for the painter Constant Troyon and some still lifes. "My dear friend" – said the latter – "you have a sense of colour, and the effect is successful, but you must take up some serious studying. Start by joining a studio where they only work on the human figure, the nude, and learn to draw."

This encouragement prompted Monet to stay in Paris, but he had no intention of frequenting the studio of Couture, where Troyon wanted to send him. Thanks to his savings and to some caricatures which he did in the cafés, he managed to make a living. He frequented the Brasserie des Martyres where he met Courbet – the leader of a group of realist painters – and Pissarro, who had already exhibited at the Salon.

After his military service and a stay in Le Havre, he returned to Paris, since his father was prepared to spend money on him as long as he dedicated himself seriously to his painting. His tutor, the painter Toulmouche, sent him to Gleyre. There, he had great influence over his fellow students and managed to persuade Bazille, Renoir and Sisley to contest the master. With them, he began to paint directly from nature in Chailly, a little village in the forest of Fontainebleau.

Success arrived in 1865 with two paintings exhibited at the Salon, but his economic resources were still very meagre. His father decided not to help him until "he will follow the righteous path of work and order." He plagued his friends, Bazille in particular, with incessant demands for money. He moved around France, looking for a way to make his fortune, and his creditors had his canvases confiscated. However, he continued to make extraordinary paintings, overflowing with light, colour and optimism. In 1865 he exhibited two landscapes at the Salon which were a great success and he undertook a very large canvas, his *Luncheon on the Grass* which, after it was damaged by humidity, he cut into three sections. He frequented the Café Guerbois, where the Batignolles group held their noisy gatherings, but participated in a very reserved manner. However, he agreed to pose for Fantin-Latour in the famous picture *The Studio of Batignolles*.

The Franco-Prussian war of 1870 took him to London, in an obscure and miserable exile which he shared with his friend Pissarro. At the end of the war and of the Commune, he returned to Paris, passing through Zaandam in Holland. In his suitcase he carried Japanese prints demonstrating novel ways of framing. In them he found ideas for a new limpidity, for a clarity of shadows and a love of synthesis. The serene atmosphere of the water lilies and irises which Monet chose to depict several times in his still lifes taken from nature (plates 19, 20, 21, 22) clearly resembles Japanese iconography.

For the rest, he had a great love for gardening all his life. In his house in Argenteuil, to which he moved after 1870, he created a garden of flowers with bright splashes of colour, where he often painted his wife, Camille, and his son, Jean. And Renoir, too, who with Sisley and Manet joined Monet at Argenteuil, painted *Madame Monet and Her Son* among the flowers in the garden. At Vétheuil, where he lived from 1878 to 1883, he also had a beautiful garden, which included a path leading to the banks of the Seine, bordered by hedges of sunflowers. *The Garden of the Artist at Vétheuil* shows a sunny refuge, far from family and financial problems, which had become customary since, even after the first impressionist exhibition organised in the studio of the photographer Nadar, Monet's economic condition remained the same.

The new bourgeoisie was more hostile to impressionist paint-

17 – Edgar Degas. *Portrait of Hortense Valpinçon* (detail) – 1869. Institute of Arts, Minneapolis.

18 – Claude Monet. *Chrysanthemums in the Form of a Fan* (detail) – 1881. Private collection.

ing than that of the Second Empire and Monet's situation became more and more precarious. He now lived with the family of Ernest Hoschédé, his old patron, an art collector and businessman who, after his bankruptcy, joined him at Vétheuil, to the south of Nantes. When Monet arrived in Vétheuil, it was late autumn. The countryside was dull and deserted, and the weather cold and sad. As his wife's health rapidly declined, Monet painted still lifes and landscapes. In spite of his increasingly worrysome economic position, he painted canvases which are a hymn of joy, like *Spring* or *Vétheuil in the Summer*.

In June 1880, the exhibition organised by Vie Moderne was a success, and he sold many paintings. He worked incessantly, attracted by the Seine, the sea, the fields and the meadows. In April 1883 he moved to Giverny, a village on the Normandy border, with Alice Hoschédé, who had become his companion. When he no longer wished to move away from his house, his garden and orchard gave him floral subjects to paint. It was at Giverny that he created the most characteristic and systematic subjects of his late works, the "series" which, until that time, he had only occasionally used. Focusing on a single point, Monet's eye became increasingly sensitive and ready to capture every variation and every infinitesimal nuance. This technique enabled him to render the duration of the impression, prolonging the moment, and giving rise to a series of impressions of various sequences of a single subject.

19 – Claude Monet. *Water Lilies* (detail) – 1907. Private collection.

Starting with the twenty canvases of the cathedral of Rouen, in 1894, Monet continued this experimentation with his series of water lilies. Towards the end of his life he recounted this experience. "There was a stream, the Ept, which comes down from Gisors to the edge of my property. I diverted it into a ditch in order to fill a little pond that I had dug in my garden and which I wanted to fill with plants. I took the catalogue and chose at random, that's all." However, the creation of this large aquatic garden had, in fact, been the result of a very carefully studied project and of the laborious tasks of draining and gardening. A bridge was constructed above the pond, which symbolised, in Japanese painting, the force which attracts and unifies the compositional elements of the landscape. What is more, it had the symbolic meaning of the "passage" from youth to maturity. The bridge, as a figurative theme, was well-loved and often depicted by the Impressionists. Monet started work in 1890 and, in that aquatic landscape that he himself had created, he soon dedicated himself to studying the effects of colour and light which he saw on the water. That same year he wrote to a friend: "I have undertaken something impossible again. Water with waving grasses in it ... It's wonderful to see, but trying to paint it is madness. I'm always struggling with this kind of problem." The first *Ponds with Water Lilies*, painted in 1899, represents the whole arch of the Japanese bridge spanning water teeming with flowering aquatic plants, with trees in the

20 – Claude Monet. *Water Lilies* (detail) – 1905. Museum of Fine Arts, bequest of Alexander Cochrane, Boston.

background. The sky can be imagined by the harmony which its light spreads over the whole setting. In 1903, Monet began to paint only the surface of the pond, without the bridge, without trees, and without ornaments. With their white, yellow, pink and sometimes light-blue flowers, supported by leaves themselves rich in pastel colours, the water lilies are arranged at different levels, from the foreground, which first attracts the eye, to the background, where the effect of perspective brings the forms closer together and softens the effect of the colours (plates 19, 20, 21, 22).

Next to the water lilies, those decadent flowers linked to the poems of Mallarmé and the preludes of Debussy, Monet

21 – Claude Monet. *Water Lilies* (detail) – 1910. Kunsthaus, Zurich.

depicts irises (plate 24), a theme which became more and more important as the influence of Japanese graphic art made its effects felt. This thin-stemmed flower, with its ornamental corolla of lanceolate leaves and its particularly slender form, appeared in many paintings. Monet was hesitant about presenting these series to the public. In May, 1909, he ex-hibited 48 *Water Lilies* painted between 1904 and 1908. They had a remarkable success and critics admired the mysteries "of water which shadow dressed and the sun undressed." In 1915, again on the same theme of water and of its reflections "now a definite obsession," Monet started a large decorative work which he offered to the French State in 1923. After his

22 – Claude Monet. *Water Lilies* (detail) – 1907. Emil Bürle Collection, Zurich.

death, and following his advice, it was placed in the two oval rooms of the Musée de l'Orangerie. "All along the walls, because of its unity, [the water lily theme] encompasses all the panels ... creating the illusion of an unending whole, of a wave with no horizon and no beach. Nerves tense from work will relax in front of this decoration, following the peaceful example of its stagnant water and, for those who live in it, this environment will offer a refuge of peaceful meditation in the middle of a flowering aquarium ..." Monet was then the last authentic survivor of the Impressionists. In 1911 Alice, his faithful companion whom he had only been able to marry in 1892, died. His sight dwindled, but he continued to paint with enthusiasm and courage until his death, on 6 December 1926.

Pierre-Auguste Renoir

Renoir was born in Limoges on 25 February 1841 into a family of artisans who, in order to improve their economic position, came to Paris in 1894. When Auguste reached working age, his parents sent him to the studio of the Lévy brothers, where he became a porcelain painter. He stayed there from 1854 to 1858, and we have preparatory drawings of roses and of bunches of flowers from that period, designed for the decoration of a plate and of a vase. Then, Renoir went to work as a decorator in a factory making fans and blinds. With the money he earned there, he decided to study painting and, in 1862, he enrolled at the Gleyre studio in the Ecole des Beaux-Arts. His very sociable character immediately prompted him to make friends with Monet, Bazille and Sisley, and it is with them that he went to paint in the forest of Fontainebleau where, until 1870, he visited several times. The first bouquets of flowers in the fields date from this period, done in a style that was still hesitating between the inspiration of Courbet and Fantin-Latour and the search for his own particular style (*Flowers in a Pot and Champagne Glass*, 1866, plate 25).

23 – Claude Monet. *Reflections on the Water* (detail) – 1917 ca. Musée Léon Alègre, Bagnols-sur-Cèze.

Renoir was already part of the Parisian artistic world, often frequenting the group which met at the Café Guerbois, led by Manet, who was considered to be the "maître." Along with Degas, Bazille, Sisley, Monet, Pissarro, Cézanne, and Fantin-Latour, there were Emile Zola, the critic Philippe Burty, the writers Duranty, Armand Sylvestre and Léo Cladel and the photographer Nadar.

It was during these meetings that the idea of a group exhibition was suggested. However, it was put off first because of the Franco-Prussian war and then because of contrasting viewpoints between the different artists and because of economic difficulties. It was only in 1874, mainly thanks to Renoir's own enthusiasm and effort, that the first exhibition took place in the studio of the photographer Nadar. What distinguished and characterised Renoir among this group of friends was his warm, sentimental participation in a subject and a great chromatic richness. The years 1864 to 1867 were those in which he was fired with passion and most ardently

24 – Claude Monet. *Iris*. Private collection.

sought new experiences, in search of his own particular style. After following Courbet, he then joined Manet, with whom he would always share a love of contemporary life.

Then, at the end of the parenthesis of war, he returned to Paris and took up painting once more, executing many still lifes (*Still Life with a Bunch of Flowers and a Fan*, of 1871; *Flowers in a Vase, Still Life with Melon, Peonies in a Vase*, of 1872). He lived modestly from the money he made by selling the paintings and sketches that he did in Parisian cafés. This impressionist period, from 1872 to 1882, is certainly the happiest period of the artist's life, in which he fully exploited the miracle of his prestigious poetic talent, making images of the world around him blossom as though in an enchanted greenhouse showing as well his mastery of all aspects of the impressionistic technique. In 1876 he met the editor Georges Charpentier and became one of the most frequent visitors at the salon of Madame Charpentier. He was

commissioned to make several family portraits, including that of *Madame Georges Charpentier and Her Daughters* (plate 30) painted in 1878, after about 40 sittings. It is a large painting in which the mistress of the house is depicted with her children Paul and Georgette and her dog Porto in the Japanese room of her mansion in Rue de Grenelle. The bamboo furniture, the Japanese painting on the wall and the vase full of flowers recreate an inner enchantment and show how fashionable Japanese art was at that time.

The Luncheon of the Boating Party (plate 29) dates from the same period, begun in the summer of 1880 and finished in his studio during the winter of 1880-81. The scene represents the end of a lively lunch. Friends of Renoir sit around the table, and on the left we see Aline Charigot, a young model, soon to become his wife. In this complex composition, Renoir paints every detail of the still life on the table, still set for lunch: bottles, glasses and bowls of

25 – Pierre-Auguste Renoir. *Flowers in a Pot and Champagne Glass* – 1866 ca. Private collection.

fruit stand out against the background of the white cloth. In 1881, tired of Paris and wishing to "renew his inspiration," he decided to leave for Algeria. That same year he visited Italy and the following year he went to Marseille. Going through a deep crisis, he decided to return to painting, following the work of Raphael and Ingres. The linear contours of his figures were then more sharply defined and their modelling became more rigorous, without, however, completely abandoning the impressionistic technique. He deepened his knowledge of painting and improved his methods, but his own fantastical world would still remain the same and the same human warmth would animate the images he painted, whether bathers or portraits, landscapes or still lifes. In 1888 he painted *The Daughters of Catulle Mendès* (plate 28), a very popular poet at that time. In this work the carefully-drawn forms exploit a play of contrasting colours, light-blue and orange-ochre, heightened by the presence of white. A dark vase of flowers on the piano enriches the scene with warm red and yellow flowers.

Renoir loved flowers, and he often added them to his most important compositions or used them as the only theme for a painting. The *Vase of Chrysanthemums* (plate 31) from the last decade of the nineteenth century, introduces us to the sumptuous colours and subjects of the Cagnes period. Red springs out in a thousand nuances, mixed with green and white in a chromatic whirl, which takes over the whole painting. It is a hymn to nature, to its richness and beauty. Renoir, forgetting that he had once deeply pondered numerous theoretical problems, has returned to colour and to Impressionism with a new vigour and strength.

He would continue to work with his new technique up to the end of the century, strengthening his bond with the sun, the colour, the light and the triumphant life of the south of France, in a vigorous and powerful song. This work can only be compared to the best of Rubens, a nickname that the friends of his youth in the porcelain factory justifiably and jokingly used for him.

He lived happily, surrounded by his family, having, at that time, a solid economic position, but he was menaced by a serious rheumatic illness and had to stop travelling. Later he

26 – Pierre-Auguste Renoir. *Still Life with Cup and Sugar Bowl* – 1904. Private collection.

30

27 – Pierre-Auguste Renoir. *Flowers in a Vase* – 1901. Private collection.

was confined to a wheelchair and eventually, as his condition worsened, he could not even hold a paintbrush in his hand. However, he continued to paint incessantly, dividing his time between Paris, Essoyes and Cagnes. At the studio he dedicated himself to still life to relax from the fatigue of his larger paintings. Although, at the beginning of his career, he concentrated on painting wild flowers, now he depicted roses (*Flowers in a Vase*, 1901, plate 27) which he used in order to study the nuances of colour that he would then apply to the feminine form, to nudes and to bathers. The works of his last period became darker and almost classical without, however, ever becoming cold or stilted. One only needs to observe the *Still Life with Cup and Sugar Bowl* (plate 26) in order to admire the pictorial charm created with such simple objects. During his old age he returned to his property at Cagnes, tortured by pain, but faithful to his work until his death on 3 December 1919.

Alfred Sisley

He was one of the first painters to participate in the impressionist movement, but he always maintained his independence, never straying from the technique he had developed with his friends during the years between 1860 and 1870. He had little happiness during his life and, sadly resigned to his lot, he dedicated himself to landscapes, only rarely painting still lifes with fruit or game.

He was born in Paris on 30 October 1839, of an English father who, in 1857, sent him to London to learn about the world of business. Instead, Sisley spent his time visiting museums and, when he returned to Paris in 1862, he obtained his father's permission to study painting. He joined the studio of Charles Gleyre where he met and became a friend of Renoir, Monet and Bazille. Every year, with his friends, he went to paint in the forest of Fontainebleau. Thanks to the money sent by his father, he did not suffer from any lack of financial resources, but after the bankruptcy of his father's firm, in 1871, he found himself suddenly penniless and was to suffer economic problems for the rest of his life.

At the beginning of his career, he painted sombre still lifes, representing fish and game. *The Pheasant* (plate 33), from 1867-68, is probably one of the masterpieces of this series of compositions. The pheasant lies on a kitchen table and the delicate tones highlight its coloured plumage and its soft down. His great talent as a painter is already evident in his study of the contrast of light and shade and his taste for creating space. Some years later he painted three or four compositions with flowers and fruit. The painting *The Lesson* is from 1871. It is a typical family scene in which he has captured his children studying. In the background, he has introduced a still life consisting of a vase full of flowers and a grandfather clock.

In 1876 he painted the *Still Life with Grapes and Nuts* which

he based on the contrast between the grey tablecloth and the red apples. This composition is formed around circular motifs and centred around the pictorial space. Delicate harmonies create the relationship between the round table, the tablecloth, the fruit and the household utensils.

Despite the poverty of his existence, Sisley continued his research in solitude, patiently awaiting a success which would only arrive after his death, from cancer, on 29 January 1899.

By way of compensation, he was the first Impressionist to receive public recognition. At the beginning of 1911, in fact, the inhabitants of Moret-sur-Loing, where Sisley had lived from 1889 until his death, opened a subscription to build a monument to his memory, which was inaugurated by the town authorities.

28 – Pierre-Auguste Renoir. *The Daughters of Catulle Mendès* – 1888. Private collection.

Camille Pissarro

Another leader of the school of Impressionism was Camille Pissarro, born on 10 July 1830 in the French colony of Saint-Thomas in the West Indies. Following the custom for members of the French bourgeoisie there, he was sent, at a very young age, to study in a college near Paris. Returning to Saint-Thomas, he started to paint as an amateur, copying the boats in the harbour. "In order to break the ties connecting me to bourgeois society," he wrote, Pissarro left his father's firm and, after two years spent wandering around Latin America, in 1855 he settled in Paris, where he frequented the Ecole des Beaux-Arts and then the Académie Suisse. In 1859 he met Monet and, two years later, Paul Cézanne, who was to have a profound influence on him.

In 1859 he moved to Pontoise, where he went to work with Cézanne. In the paintings from this period, he abandoned the large bituminous shadows of Courbet; his palette became clearer and his colours brighter. Particularly after his stay in London, where he had taken refuge during the Franco-Prussian war, and where he worked with Monet, his colours give the impression of diffused light. However, when compared to other members of the group, we see that his paintings always maintain a clear and well-defined composition, with a constant and balanced structure. His affinity to Cézanne must have played an important role since, on two occasions, in 1874-75 and in 1877, he was Cézanne's guest at Pontoise. Although he had fully participated in the trials and tribulations of the movement, Pissarro's painting never betrayed the

30 – Pierre-Auguste Renoir. *Madame Georges Charpentier and Her Daughters* – 1878. The Metropolitan Museum of Art, Wolfe Fund, New York.

premises on which it was founded. He always considered it essential to work slowly and thoughtfully when creating a painting. However, his life was inextricably linked to that of the Impressionists. He actively took part in all the exhibitions, until 1886, the eighth collective exhibition, and tried to attenuate the friction and rivalries between them and to maintain the unity of the group in any way he could. He had serious economic difficulties (he had six children), but this in no way affected his artistic production.

After meeting Seurat and Signac in 1885, he was fired with enthusiasm for Pointillism, a pictorial genre which he aban-

doned five years later in order to return to a "less scientific" type of painting. During the last years of his life, eye problems prevented him from painting in the open-air, so he made studies of landscapes from behind window panes and several still lifes that are full of optimism. In *Roses from Nice* (plate 15), which he painted in 1902, when his eye troubles had made him almost blind, he uses a bold brushstroke, attentive to the vibrations of light and shade and to the constructive solidity of the composition.

He continued to work, although half blind, until his death, on 13 November 1903.

Paul Cézanne

Cézanne dedicated all his strength, all his dreams, all his inventive talent and his productive skill to the service of painting. Throughout his life he was haunted by a sole desire to paint, and he compared himself to an almond tree, bearing its fruit every season.

He was born in Aix-en-Provence on 19 January 1839, into a wealthy family from Cesana Turinoise. He followed regular school studies and was a school friend of Emile Zola, with whom he had a deep friendship which lasted until 1882. At seventeen he started to study drawing, following courses given by Joseph Gilbert. Despite fierce opposition from his father, he obtained permission to study painting full-time and, in 1871, joined his friend Emile Zola in Paris. Discouraged by the impact of the capital city, he returned to Aix, determined to return to studying law once again and to work in his father's bank. However, his vocation as a painter was too strong. He returned to Paris, this time for good, spending half his time in the north and half in the south of France.

He met Pissarro at the Académie Suisse and they immediately became friends, having a similar character and similar aspirations. At that time he frequented the Louvre and discovered nature through the eyes of his impressionist friends. He was not to take up their style of painting spontaneously, "as a bird sings." His art, wrought with conflict, developed in a succession of periods of hope and discouragement.

Until 1872 he remained tied to his predisposition for con-trasts in black and white (*The Black Clock*). The *Still Life with Skull and Chandelier* (plate 50), dating from 1865-67, also belongs to his dark period. In his romantic conception, the skull, the candle, the book, and the faded flowers symbolise human transience, a *memento mori*. When one is young, the skull can in some way be interpreted as an obsessive fear of death, and this returns, among the flowers, in the *Still Life with Skull*, painted between 1895 and 1900, when Cézanne seemed to have recovered from that sombre melancholia which made him fascinated by images of crime and death.

Still life was one of Cézanne's favourite themes and a subject he used throughout his career as an artist, during his romantic, impressionist and constructivist periods. One is surprised by the deliberate disorder of the objects in his compositions, the result of careful and meticulous preparation. The subject is always seen from a heightened viewpoint, in a vision which would collapse if it were not the result of a perfect balance of relationships between the various elements of the composition.

His favourite form of expression is colour. The canvas *Three Apples* (plate 49), dating from around 1872, is essentially based on chromatic relationships. The three apples, arranged simply on a light canvas with pronounced folds, are illuminated and acquire solidity thanks to touches of pure colour. In fact, this type of painting takes its meaning from the different tones of colour.

Innate suspicion prevented Cézanne from spontaneously tak-

31 – Pierre-Auguste Renoir.
Vase of Chrysanthemums.
Musée des Beaux-Arts, Rouen.

32 – Alfred Sisley. *Still Life:
Apples and Grapes* – 1876.
Sterling and Francine Clark Art
Institute, Williamstown (Mass.).

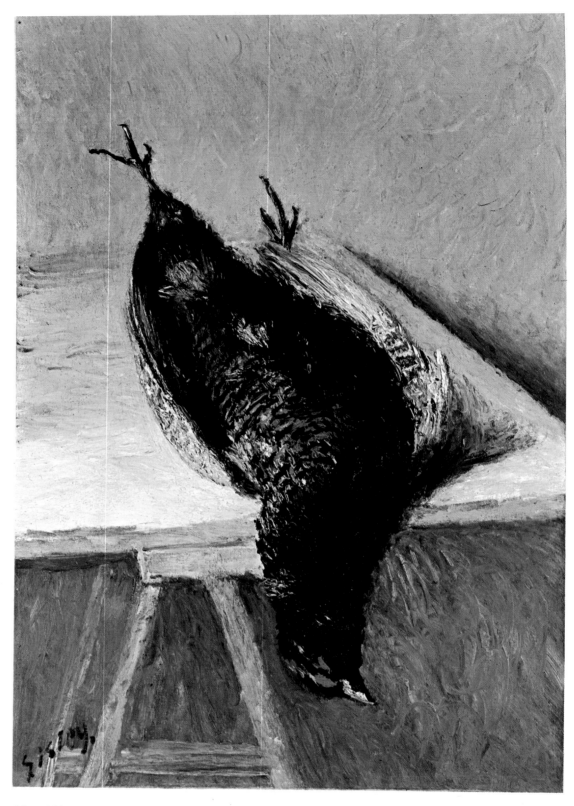

33 – Alfred Sisley. *The Pheasant* – 1867-68. Private collection.

34 – Paul Gauguin. *Still Life with Flowers and an Idol.*
Private collection.

ing up impressionist painting. However, in 1872, he accepted the invitation of Pissarro (who lived in Pontoise) and went to live for two years in Auvers-sur-Seine. There he embarked on his impressionist period. He worked with Pissarro in the open air – although unwilling to do so – and agreed to lighten his palette. He understood by artistic intuition that it was not enough to represent objects with the simplicity with which they appear to the naked eye. He was reluctant to depict objects disappearing into the atmosphere and rendered by fine brush-strokes. The problem of outlining already obsessed him. Thus he made his paintings using little touches of colour, gradually creating a pleasant shading effect and then structuring these zones into more complex groups, forming more general subjects.

In *Table Set for a Meal* (plate 53), of 1875-76, he multiplied the variety of tones. The dining table, overflowing with objects arranged in a conventional fashion, was later replaced by a kitchen table. He worked slowly. For his still lifes he used paper flowers instead of real ones, which faded even before the painting was underway. During his Argentueil period, he showed a predilection for vases of flowers. He made two versions of the painting *Bouquet of Flowers in a Vase*, one of which is now at the Hermitage Museum in St. Petersburg and the other at the Louvre. His still lifes, still geometrically conceived, reveal his wish to create multiple variations in tone, in order to obtain a vibrant and sonorous effect.

In the *Still Life with Apples, Biscuits and a Bottle* and in his *Apples and Biscuits* (plate 57), both from around 1877, Cézanne tackled circumferences, ovals and cones and the regular parallelepipeds of biscuits on a plate. In the first of the two, the suppleness of the tablecloth is rendered by a play of angles and triangles. Cézanne freely distributed the objects in the manner of the Primitivists. In the newspaper *L'Impres-*

35 – Paul Gauguin. *Mandolin and Pot of Flowers* – 1883. Private collection.

36 – Paul Gauguin. *Roses and Statuette* – 1890 ca. Musée de Saint-Denis, Reims.

37 – Paul Gauguin.
Asters on a Bureau
(detail) – 1886.
Private collection.

38 – Paul Gauguin. *Van Gogh Painting Sunflowers at Arles* – 1888. Vincent van Gogh Foundation, Amsterdam.

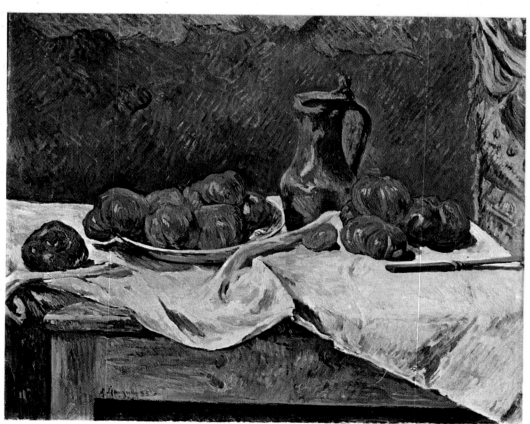

39 – Paul Gauguin. *Still Life with Tomatoes* – 1883. Private collection.

40 – Vincent van Gogh. *Still Life with Five Bottles and Cup* – 1884-85. Rijksmuseum Kröller-Müller, Otterlo.

sioniste, Georges Rivière wrote about Cézanne that "his still lifes, so beautiful and so exact in their tonal relationship, have something solemn about them. In all his paintings the artist is moved, since he experiences in nature the same violent emotion that his skill transmits to the canvas."

Georges Rivière wrote those words on the occasion of the third impressionist exhibition in 1877, to which Cézanne contributed 17 canvases (still lifes and landscapes), which some critics started to view with a certain sympathy.

Between 1878 and 1882, during a period of solitary meditation, Cézanne felt the necessity to achieve a greater synthesis of balance in his compositions and he reduced the forms to their essential terms. A still life from the period 1879-82, from a private collection in Paris, illustrates how this problem would be resolved. It is a painting which greatly influenced the Post-Impressionists. In 1890 Gauguin reproduced it in the *Portrait of Marie Lagadu* (The Art Institute of Chicago) as did Maurice Denis in *Hommage to Cézanne* of 1900 (Musée National d'Art Moderne of Paris).

In 1878, Cézanne moved to Estaque. His impressionist experiences had by then become problematic for the artist, being opposed to his manner of conception. He wished to overcome them in order to strengthen his own conception, his own personal vision of the world, reached in solitary meditation and with a desire for "construction in search of nature." Landscapes and still lifes reduced to their essential forms are reconstructed in simple, geometrical figures, with a purity of images and volumes and with a fantastic and structured vibration of colour (*Glass and Pears*, 1879-82, plate 52).

Towards 1888-90 his art achieved a total mastery over its methods, with an ever greater and truer simplicity, typically in contrast with the more tormented character of his previous

45

41 – Vincent van Gogh. *Sunflowers* – 1887. The Metropolitan Museum of Art, Roger Fund, 1949, New York.

works. He still worked slowly (in fact he never dated his works and it is even now difficult to date them with any precision). His moody character did not help. He only found peace when he was middle-aged, being used to the deceptions and doubts that he had always felt about his own worth.

In the still lifes of this period he no longer worked towards geometry but started from a geometrical viewpoint, which then allowed him to forget about it. Having perfectly assimilated the geometry, he kept it in mind, which was enough to animate his work without suffocating it and without letting the mechanism supporting the composition become overpowering. In *Still Life with Plaster Cupid* (plate 54), of 1885, Cézanne maintained the elements of a severe, pyramidal composition, which was so dear to him, with the image of a plaster cast statuette in the centre. The structural organisation and the geometrical scansion of space are still founded on a sharp chromatic sensitivity.

Cézanne needed no particular objects in order to express himself. In the canvas *Plaster Cupid* (plate 55), of 1895, he collected everyday objects and one has the impression of looking with him at the table of fruit – pears and apples beside the little plaster statuette of Eros – and beyond, to the folded blue curtain and the piece of furniture against the back wall.

Here, above all, Cézanne used an association of colours. The blue of the wall, of the furniture, the curtain and of Eros, the yellowish-red of the fruit on the ochre-coloured table and the touches of yellow applied to the blue of the furniture, all highlight the intensity of the colour. All the objects are situated a little below eye-height. Therefore the spectator sees the scene as though standing in the same position as the painter.

During the last ten years of his life, Cézanne increasingly appreciated being alone and his character became increasingly bitter. Old before his time, probably because he suffered from diabetes, and always agitated, he was continually moving house. However, as his fame increased, he received numerous demonstrations of admiration, both from the public and from the critics, encouraging him to maintain a frenetic pace of activity, lasting until his death in 1906. His search for luminosity and transparency made him give great importance to watercolours, as in the admirable virtuosity of *Jacket on a Stool* (plate 56).

The still lifes of his last ten years acquired a greater splendour and magnificence than he had ever previously achieved, and Cézanne, while affirming the autonomy of his means, also strengthened the autonomy of his vision.

42 – Vincent van Gogh. *Vase with Sunflowers* – 1889. Rijksmuseum Vincent van Gogh, Amsterdam.

43 – Vincent van Gogh. *Vase with Carnations and Gillyflowers* – 1890. Private collection.

Still Life with Fruit and Pitcher (plate 51), dating from 1895-1900, is seen from several different angles in order to emphasise the volumetric structure of the objects. Variations of perspective and angle would become one of the motifs which later inspired cubist painting. Cézanne continued to work with no respite until his death. Surprised by a storm while he was painting in the open air, he suffered a stroke and died on 22 October.

Still Life and Post-Impressionist Painting: Paul Gauguin
Cézanne's influence on the art of his successors was immense and irreplaceable. His immediate successors, and those first

influenced by him, can be best represented by Gauguin. Although he had a strong personality which was inevitably opposed to that of Cézanne, Gauguin's predilection for composition could not remain unaffected by the anti-impressionist discoveries of his predecessor. Making contact with the Impressionists after their first and most difficult battles had already taken place, Gauguin did not wish to subscribe to a revolution which was not his own, experiencing a need for escape and originality which made him feel very detached.

Paul Gauguin was born in Paris on 7 June 1848. With his parents – in 1849 his father, opposing Louis-Napoleon Bonaparte, was forced to leave France for Peru, his wife's native country – he led an errant existence from the first months of his life. After the death of his father, in 1855, his mother returned to France and settled in Orleans. Passionate and full of imagination like his mother, Gauguin's life was marked by exoticism and a proud independence. The social status of his family conditioned his choice of work. He sailed for several years in the Atlantic and the Pacific and fought the war of 1870 in the Marines. On his return, he followed the advice of his tutor and went to work for a stock-broker. He lived a very bourgeois life and seemed to appreciate its tranquillity. He married a young Danish girl who would give him five children. He learnt to draw and started to paint for pleasure.

44 – Vincent van Gogh. *Chestnut Blossoms* – 1890. Emile Bürle Collection, Zurich.

46 – Vincent van Gogh. *Still Life with Onions and Drawing Table* – 1889. Rijksmuseum Kröller-Müller, Otterlo.

His tutor introduced him to Pissarro, who awakened his memories of the exotic, and who was, indeed, generally full of advice for young painters. He became interested in the impressionist movement and also bought some of their canvases. His technique improved and his first still lifes demonstrate a classicism in his instinct for painting.

From 1880 onwards, he regularly participated in the impressionist group. Recommended by Pissarro, he took part in their fourth exhibition. Sisley and Monet then refused to present their own works. "The little church has become a banal school, opening its doors to the first dauber of canvases," Monet declared to the press, alluding to Gauguin. The latter

45 – Vincent van Gogh. *Wild Flowers in a Vase* – 1888 (?). Private collection.

was, however, no longer an amateur painter and seemed to hold a precise position among the impressionist painters. What he found in this new technique is even more evident in the still lifes: the search for a simple, apparently improvised, arrangement; the importance of the general atmosphere and, above all, of light; the conservation of the natural character of things.

Increasingly dominated by his passion for painting, in 1883 he left the stock exchange. Moreover, after the financial crash he hoped to gain new resources from painting and he insisted in his decision even when his economic situation worsened. He settled in Rouen, hoping to find better possibilities and better living conditions. The two still lifes, *Mandolin and Pot of Flowers* (plate 35) and *Still Life with Tomatoes* (plate 39), date from this period, the latter reminiscent in its composition and in the rounded form of the vegetables of similar paintings

51

47 – Vincent van Gogh. *Van Gogh's Chair and Pipe* – 1888. The Tate Gallery, London.

by Cézanne. His material difficulties increased, and after an attempt to find work in Denmark, he separated from his wife, returning to France very poor but increasingly convinced to dedicate his life to painting. He even accepted work as a billsticker.

The year 1886 brought no economic improvement in his situation, although he presented 18 canvases at the eighth impressionist exhibition. *Asters on a Bureau* (plate 37) dates from that year, a still life in soberly harmonious shades,

lightened by the white vase. On the right, there is a little Peruvian idol which he inserted into many paintings at that time, including the *Still Life with a Profile of Laval*. On the canvas, an idol and apples, showing Cézanne's influence, are resting on a white tablecloth and are observed by his friend Charles Laval, who was to become his travelling companion on his first trip to Martinique. In fact, in 1887, he decided to try his luck outside the civilised world. With Laval, he travelled first to Panama and then to Martinique.

"In order to constantly increase my celebrity, I even spend three consecutive days without eating. What I want to do, above all, is to leave Paris, which is a desert for a poor man." He came back from his stay in Martinique with paintings already showing the characteristics which would be peculiar to his art, even constituting a new style. In many paintings from that period, we see a dark outline around his forms, contrary to impressionist ideas. His palette is simplified and he uses warm and more brutal tones in the contrasts.

His painting seems to be moving away from a spontaneous and improvised art to a more organised form, towards compositions assembled according to the whim of the artist.

The year 1888 was decisive for Gauguin's art. From that time, the painter directed himself towards clearly delineated forms and large surfaces of uniform colour. He applied this technique more systematically at the end of the year, during his stay in Arles with van Gogh. "That year", he said later, "I sacrificed everything, technique and colour, to style, because I wanted to force myself to do something different from what I normally do."

In October he had joined his friend van Gogh, who had invited Gauguin to live at his house in Provence. Despite reciprocal esteem and admiration, cohabitation proved difficult and finished dramatically. In December 1888 Gauguin left Arles and returned to Brittany, to Pont-Aven.

In Arles he learnt to insert human figures, even into paintings which started as landscapes. In fact, he even depicted *Van Gogh Painting Sunflowers at Arles* (plate 38). The painter, the flowers and all the forms are outlined and well-defined by a line delineating each precise zone of colour. The basic shades, browns, ochres and green, stand out in their relationship to the light and dark blue. Gauguin particularly admired van Gogh's *Sunflowers* and this painting also pays homage to his friend.

The still lifes of 1888-89 clearly show Cézanne's influence. In the portrait of Marie Lagadu, of 1890, he used a still life by Cézanne as a background and, like Cézanne, he painted apples. With their full, rounded forms, the apples became an object in themselves, clearly defined and sculpted forms, and no longer haphazardly chosen accessories, making them the main focus of the picture.

The paintings made during his stay in Brittany show a desire

48 – Vincent van Gogh. *Gauguin's Chair* – 1888. Rijksmuseum Vincent van Gogh, Amsterdam.

for exoticism, and it was during this period that Gauguin inserted representations of small Peruvian idols into his paintings, such as in *Roses and Statuette* (plate 36) and in *Still Life with Flowers and an Idol* (plate 34).

The artist had been thinking of leaving France and forming a "Tropical Studio" for several months. "I'll go to Haiti, and hope to spend the rest of my days there. I think that the art that you appreciate in me is only the seed of what I could cultivate within myself out there, in primitive and savage surroundings," he wrote in 1890 to Odilon Redon.

At the beginning of April 1891, having collected the money necessary for his trip and for his accommodation through a public sale of his works, he embarked for Tahiti. It was not a retreat, but a voluntary departure to find a different way of living. However, he did not manage to rid himself of the civilised world: "It was Europe with the addition of colonial snobbism," he wrote from Noa-Noa. Thus he settled in the most isolated spots, by the sea. No money arrived from France and illness added to his financial worries. Therefore Gauguin decided to return to France. In May 1893 the Minister of the Interior paid for his repatriation. In Paris he lived with a Javanese national in an exotically decorated studio, strangely furnished, where he received the best artists and poets of the time, but was beset by further deceptions and worries.

At the end of 1894 Gauguin took an "irrevocable decision to leave forever, for Oceania." He organised a new public sale of his works and, embarking from Marseilles, he reached Papeete on 1 September 1895. Further economic problems added once more to his health problems, and his situation got progressively worse. Then he tried to commit suicide. Works he had painted in Tahiti helped him to enter further into the spirit of the natives, trying to understand their religion and their legends. All this was heightened by the elegiac landscapes of natural simplicity. His still lifes also contain the richness and scope of his more important works, to the point that the fruit and other objects are treated as definitive things, like buildings or monuments.

After leaving Tahiti to settle in the Marquesas Islands, Gauguin seemed to have found what he had been looking for – primitive life. Finally he was at his ease and his art demonstrates that calm and intimate communion between man and

49 – Paul Cézanne. *Three Apples* – 1872 ca. Private collection.

nature. He ended his days in the Marquesas Islands, where he died on 8 May 1803. Three years later, at the Salon d'Automne in Paris, 227 of his works were exhibited in a large retrospective exhibition. It marked the end of a long tragedy and the beginning of a lasting triumph.

Vincent van Gogh

"What did he not do to learn to draw, to draw according to his vision and to the reality of things. I still see him at Cormon, in the afternoon ... sitting opposite a copy of an ancient work, copying the beautiful forms with the patience of an angel. He tried to reproduce the outlines, shapes and the perspective. He corrected, started again with passion, and rubbed out until he rubbed a hole in the page.

In fact he never suspected, when confronted with this Latin marvel, that it totally opposed his Dutch nature, which he wished to conquer. And he would find his way much faster and better among those Impressionists with their free imagination and easy lyricism than in that calm perfection, revealed to peaceful men, during the civilisations close to nature and thought. How quickly Vincent will understand all this! And then he left Cormon." This episode, recounted by Emile Bernard, dates from May 1886. In February Vincent van Gogh had joined his brother Théo who managed the Goupil Gallery in Montmartre in Paris, and who represented for him not only his family but also his only contact with the Parisian artistic world, in full evolution at that time. Vincent already had years of suffering and hard work behind him.

He was the eldest of five children, born on 30 March 1853 at Groot Zundert, in Dutch Brabant, and was the son of a Protestant minister. At sixteen he started work as a salesman at The Hague, in his uncles' art gallery. In 1873, he moved to

51 – Paul Cézanne. *Still Life with Fruit and Pitcher* – 1895-1900. Musée du Louvre, Paris.

the London branch of the gallery where he stayed for two years, until he was transferred to Paris once more. Attracted by both ancient and modern painting, he attended exhibitions and public sales, visited museums and became so disinterested in his work that he would be forced to leave it. Théo advised him to concentrate solely on painting, but Vincent did not yet know what he wanted to do. He read, drew, and was filled with religious exaltation. He returned to London, which had greatly impressed him, and became an assistant preacher in a sordid area. After unsuccessfully trying to enter

the faculty of theology in Amsterdam and, obsessed with religion, he joined the miners at Borinage, one of the saddest and poorest areas of Belgium, in order to exercise his evangelism directly.

He was to come out of this experience a changed man. However, it was in Borinage that he decided to take up his career of painting and to publicise, through his paintings, the miserable life of the poor. His brother Théo helped him economically. He started his studies in a very disorderly fashion. He practised with manuals, studied anatomy and

52 – Paul Cézanne. *Glass and Pears* – 1879-82. Private collection.

perspective in Brussels and in the winter of 1881 he stayed with his cousin Mauve, a painter, in The Hague.
One of the rare paintings we have of his stay in The Hague is *Cultivation of Flowers in Holland*, from the spring of 1883. This detailed representation of a field of flowers reminds one of the precision of the Flemish masters, contrasting with the calligraphic rendering of the silhouettes of trees, typical of Japanese art. The lively profusion of flowers and the dark houses of the farmers reflect van Gogh's early interest for subjects that he will continue to treat throughout his career.
His tragic love for a prostitute and economic difficulties prompted him to leave The Hague and rejoin his family, after a stay at the Dronthe, the northern equivalent of Barbizon.
At Neuen, a village near Eindhoven where he stayed from 1883 until the winter of 1885, he was in a permanent state of exaltation. Possessed by his passion for painting, he scandalised his fellow citizens by his anti-conventional behaviour and argued with his family. There he executed about 250 drawings and, following Millet's example, he made two important series, one dedicated to peasant life and the other to that of weavers. Ignoring Théo's advice, by then convinced of the value of the luminosity of impressionist paintings, he limited his palette to bistres and browns, suited to the scenes of poverty he depicted, such as *The Potato-Eaters*, his most important work during this period. At a goldsmiths' in Eindhoven he found motifs for still lifes which allowed him to

experiment with pictorial techniques, inspired by the ancient Dutch masters. He chose familiar household objects which answered the needs of peasant life: bottles, pots, mortars and cups, as in the *Still Life with Five Bottles and Cup* (plate 40) painted between November 1884 and March 1885.
At Neuen he was to experience both family and sentimental crises, his mother's serious illness and the death of his father, and the attempted suicide of a young girl whom he had refused. All this added to his economic problems and prompted him to rejoin his brother Théo in Paris. During the journey there, he stopped at Anvers where he discovered Japanese prints and the work of Rubens, which he studied in churches and museums.
In February 1886 Vincent was in Paris, with Théo. He immediately enrolled at the studio of Cormon where he met Toulouse-Lautrec and, thanks to his brother, also met the impressionist painters who, on 16 May, held the eighth exhibition of the group. He was particularly impressed by Pissarro, thanks to whom he was able to participate in the neo-impressionist experience, and by Gauguin, who dominated him from the first with his personality and the power and grandeur of his work.
Having left Cormon's studio, he started to paint views of Paris and self-portraits and, above all, concentrated his efforts on still lifes, and representing familiar objects and bunches of flowers in brilliant colours. "I paint almost exclu-

sively flowers, to get used to using colours different from grey, that is, pink, light or bright green, sky blue, mauve, yellow, orange, and a good red," he wrote to his sister. In a little garden in Montmartre he discovered sunflowers and painted them as a bright, moving mass, with their crown of tongues of fire (plate 41). His Parisian years, during which he was able to deepen his experiences in the direction of Avant-Garde painting, of Divisionism, and of synthesis, were the happiest in his tormented existence.

Meanwhile, he secretly prepared for his departure for the south of France. Théo was about to get married and he was worried about being a burden to him. On Toulouse-Lautrec's advice he left for Arles on 20 February 1880. When he arrived, Provence was covered with snow, but, in the spring, the clear sky and budding plants made him feel he had found paradise, the ideal place to establish the "house of friends" that he dreamed of. "The countryside seems as beautiful as Japan in the clarity of its atmosphere and its joyous effects of colour," he wrote to his friend Emile Bernard. In the summer, he painted in the sunlight in cornfields. He had left behind the changing colours and the nuances of Impressionism and he used more violent hues, well aware that "time will make them all too soft." On 20 October 1888 Gauguin joined him, the first guest of the "house of friends." The landscape,

the light and the colours charmed the two painters in the same way. From an artistic point of view, their life together was very profitable. Gauguin painted van Gogh's portrait as he painted his famous picture *Sunflowers* (plate 38), with the flowers placed beside his easel.

Gauguin admired the works of van Gogh, especially the sunflowers, which Vincent painted both in full bloom and faded, hanging their heads. He felt a special affinity for these flowers because their bright yellow colour characterised the south.

He wrote to his brother Théo: "Gauguin told me the other day that he had seen a painting of sunflowers by Claude Monet, sunflowers in a large, very beautiful Japanese vase – but that he preferred mine ... If, when I am forty, I can make a painting of figures as good as that of the flowers which pleased Gauguin, there'll be a place for me alongside any other artist. Therefore, I shall persevere."

Yellow is the fundamental colour in the Arles works. The facade of the house in which he lived was yellow, as was, inside the house, the decoration of a series of canvases representing sunflowers, symbol of the burning sun of the Midi. In *Vase with Sunflowers* (plate 42), painted in January 1889, the yellow reaches an orange intensity and its nuances are multiplied until they tend towards green. A fine green line

53 – Paul Cézanne. *Table Set for a Meal* – 1875-76 (?). Private collection.

54 – Paul Cézanne. *Still Life Plaster Cupid* – 1885 ca. Courtauld Institute Galleries, London.

55 – Paul Cézanne. *Plaster Cupid* – 1895 ca. National Museum, Stockholm.

sketches the volume of the vase and the signature. In this series, in which he paints the same flowers whether in bud or dishevelled, the dominant yellow takes all possible forms. He had great difficulty in finding models. "I've made, in my own way again, a picture of my bedroom. Well, I really enjoyed painting this interior without anything, with the simplicity of Seurat."

He writes again to his brother Théo: "My last studies are rather strange, a wooden, straw-bottomed chair, entirely yellow on red bricks, leaning against the wall (in daytime). Then Gauguin's chair, red and green, a nocturnal effect, the wall

and floor also red and green, on the seat, two novels and a candle."

Van Gogh's Chair and Pipe (plate 47) and *Gauguin's Chair* (plate 48) were painted in December 1888, before Gauguin left Arles and van Gogh's house because of their continual arguments. The objects chosen, and sometimes used for long series, no doubt have symbolic significance. Much time has been spent in search of explanations: the empty chair, full of a sense of absence, and the shoes of the eternal traveller, left in a corner, seem to be the obsessions of a man in search of the impossible.

56 – Paul Cézanne. *Jacket on a Stool* – 1890-95. Marianne Feilchnfeldt Collection, Zurich.

Despite reciprocal admiration and esteem, their two characters were constantly in conflict. Gauguin was hard, intransigent, obsessed with a desire to translate what he saw in a synthetic and symbolic form. Van Gogh was passionately impulsive, urged on by his obsession for capturing light in the bright colours of his canvases. The continuous arguments exhausted the fragile nerves of van Gogh, who, on the night of 23 December, threw himself at his friend with a razor and then, to punish himself, cut off his ear and offered it to a prostitute. Hospitalised at Saint-Paul, van Gogh was dismissed on 7 January, apparently cured. "I've started work again and I already have three finished canvases at the studio, plus a portrait of Monsieur Rey [the doctor who looked after him], that I've given him as a souvenir ... I feel a little weak, a little anxious and impressionable," he wrote on 10 January to his brother, with whom he kept up a daily correspondence. "Work distracts me. I need to be distracted," he wrote ten days later. His short stay in Arles had been his most prolific period as a painter, a period in which his works had reached their splendour. In little less than a year he had painted around 200 pictures and made a hundred drawings, intense and homogeneous masterpieces inspired by everyday subjects, taken from the café tables he frequented, the simple furniture of his room, or the objects on his table.

On 3 May 1889 van Gogh voluntarily decided to enter the psychiatric hospital of Saint-Rémy where he was to spend a year, painting 150 canvases and making around a hundred drawings. He worked in the garden of the hospital, where he found inspiration to paint flowers, irises, lilacs, and oleanders. Sometimes he went through crises and periods of helplessness and had to stop working. Then he would start working again, perfectly his own master. Worried about his brother's health, Théo decided to take him to Paris, but the noise and agitation of the city tired the painter. Doctor Gachet agreed to treat him, and, on 21 May 1890, Vincent moved to Auvers-sur-Oise. "Here there is a lot to draw," he wrote to his brother. Gachet, a personal friend of Pissarro and Cézanne, taught him the technique of etching and allowed him to work at his house in his large garden. At Auvers, van Gogh painted flowers again. He used soft hues, a range of colours in which the tonalities balanced and contrasted with each other. In *Chestnut Blossoms* (plate 44), a canvas painted before 25 May, the painter exploited a rather cold canvas, in tones of grey, by livening it up with blues and gleams of red and yellow in the chestnut flowers. Particularly in the canvas *Vase with Carnations and Gillyflowers* (plate 43), in June, the asymmetry and angularity contrasted directly with the rounded forms of the table. It is a still life full of vigour, a tangle of forms and colours.

Two months after his arrival in Auvers, he started hallucinating again. A few days before shooting himself through the heart, he wrote to his brother: "In my work my life is at risk and my mind has been half consumed." He died two days later, on 29 July, in the arms of his brother Théo.

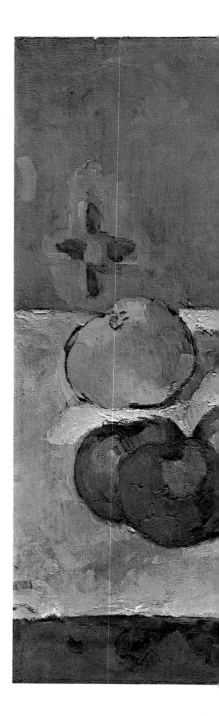

57 – Paul Cézanne. *Apples and Biscuits* – 1877. Private collection.

Editor in chief Anna Maria Mascheroni

Art director Ettore Maiotti

Text Simonetta Venturi

Translation Joelle Crowle

Production Art, Bologna

Photo credits Gruppo Editoriale Fabbri S.p.A., Milan

Copyright © 1990 by Gruppo Editoriale Fabbri S.p.A., Milan

Published by Park Lane
An Imprint of Grange Books Ltd
The Grange
Grange Yard
LONDON
SE1 3AG

ISBN 1-85627-244-3

This edition published 1993

Printed in Italy by Gruppo Editoriale Fabbri S.p.A., Milan